Compassion and the Individual

Tenzin Gyatso
the Fourteenth
Dalai Lama

Wisdom Publications • Boston

First published 1991, 10,000 copies
Reprinted   1992, 46,000 copies
              1994, 15,000 copies

WISDOM PUBLICATIONS
361 Newbury Street
Boston
Massachusetts 02115
United States of America

© Tenzin Gyatso, the Fourteenth Dalai Lama 1991

ISBN 0 86171 079 7

10 9 8 7 6 5 4

Cover photo courtesy of James Weng

Wisdom Publications is both honored and delighted to make available for free distribution around the world, this and other booklets by His Holiness the Dalai Lama, such as A Human Approach to World Peace (65,000 copies in print), The Global Community and the Need for Universal Responsibility (15,000 copies), and Words of Truth: A Prayer for Peace in Tibet and Compassion in the World (7,000 copies). Tens of thousands more copies of most of these booklets are also in print in many different languages.

Our ability to publish and distribute such booklets depends solely upon your kindness and help. Donations—tax-deductible in the USA—may be sent to Wisdom at the above address, and we thank most sincerely the sponsors of this and the other booklets we have produced in the past. Please let us know if you would like to join with us in spreading His Holiness's message of peace, compassion, and wisdom to all people everywhere.

Typeset in Goudy Old Style and printed at
Eurasia Press, Singapore

The purpose of life

ONE GREAT QUESTION underlies our experience, whether we think about it consciously or not: What is the purpose of life? I have considered this question and would like to share my thoughts in the hope that they may be of direct, practical benefit to those who read them.

I believe that the purpose of life is to be happy. From the moment of birth, every human being wants happiness and does not want suffering. Neither social conditioning nor education nor ideology affect this. From the very core of our being, we simply desire contentment. I don't know whether the universe, with its countless galaxies, stars and planets, has a deeper meaning or not, but at the very least, it is clear that we humans who live on this earth face the task of making a happy life for ourselves. Therefore, it is important to discover what will bring about the greatest degree of happiness.

How to achieve happiness

For a start, it is possible to divide every kind of happiness and suffering into two main categories: mental and physical. Of the two, it is the mind that exerts the greatest influence on most of us. Unless we are either gravely ill or deprived of basic necessities, our physical condition plays a secondary role in life. If the body is content, we virtually ignore it. The mind, however, registers every event, no matter how small. Hence we should devote our most serious efforts to bringing about mental peace.

From my own limited experience I have found that the greatest degree of inner tranquillity comes from the development of love and compassion.

The more we care for the happiness of others, the greater our own sense of well-being becomes. Cultivating a close, warm-hearted feeling for others automatically puts the mind at ease. This helps remove whatever fears or insecurities we may have and gives us the strength to cope with any obstacles we encounter. It is the ultimate source of success in life.

As long as we live in this world we are bound to encounter problems. If, at such times, we lose hope and become discouraged, we diminish our ability to face difficulties. If, on the other hand, we remember that it is not just ourselves but everyone who has to undergo suffering, this more realistic perspective will increase our determination and capacity to overcome troubles. Indeed, with this attitude, each new obstacle can be seen as yet another valuable opportunity to improve our mind!

Thus we can strive gradually to become more compassionate, that is we can develop both genuine sympathy for others' suffering and the will to help remove their pain. As a result, our own serenity and inner strength will increase.

Our need for love

Ultimately, the reason why love and compassion bring the greatest happiness is simply that our nature cherishes them above all else. The need for love lies at the very foundation of human existence. It results from the profound interdependence we all share with one another. However capable and skillful an individual may be, left alone, he or she will not survive. However vigorous and independent one may feel during the most prosperous periods of life, when one is sick or very young or very old, one must depend on the support of others.

Interdependence, of course, is a fundamental law of nature. Not only higher forms of life but also many of the smallest insects are social beings who, without any religion, law or education, survive by mutual cooperation based on an innate recognition of their interconnectedness. The most subtle level of material phenomena is also governed by interdependence. All phenomena, from the planet we inhabit to the oceans, clouds, forests and flowers that surround us, arise in dependence upon subtle patterns of energy. Without their proper interaction, they dissolve and decay.

It is because our own human existence is so dependent on the help of others that our need for love lies at the very foundation of our existence. Therefore we need a genuine sense of responsibility and a sincere concern for the welfare of others.

We have to consider what we human beings really are. We are not like machine-made objects. If we were merely mechanical entities, then machines themselves could alleviate all of our sufferings and fulfil our needs. However, since we are not solely material creatures, it is a mistake to place all our hopes for happiness on external development alone. Instead, we should consider our origins and nature to discover what we require.

Leaving aside the complex question of the creation and evolution of our universe, we can at least agree that each of us is the product of our own parents. In general, our conception took place not just in the context of sexual desire but from our parents' decision to have a child. Such decisions are founded on responsibility and altruism — the parents' compassionate commitment to care for their child until it is able to take care of itself. Thus, from the very moment of our conception, our parents' love is directly involved in our creation.

Moreover, we are completely dependent upon our mother's care from the earliest stages of our growth. According to some scientists, a pregnant woman's mental state, be it calm or agitated, has a direct physical effect on her unborn child.

The expression of love is also very important at the time of birth. Since the very first thing we do is suck milk from our mother's breast, we naturally feel close to her, and she must feel love for us in order to feed us properly; if she feels anger or resentment her milk may not flow freely.

Then there is the critical period of brain development from the time of birth up to at least the age of three or four, during which time loving physical contact is the single most important factor for the normal growth of the child. If the child is not held, hugged, cuddled or loved, its development will be impaired and its brain will not mature properly.

Since a child cannot survive without the care of others, love is its most important nourishment. The happiness of childhood, the allaying of the child's many fears and the healthy development of its self-confidence all depend directly upon love.

Nowadays, many children grow up in unhappy homes. If they do not receive proper affection, in later life they will rarely love their parents and, not infrequently, will find it hard to love others. This is very sad.

As children grow older and enter school, their need for support must be met by their teachers. If a teacher not only imparts academic education but also assumes rsponsibility for preparing students for life, his or her pupils will feel trust and respect and what has been taught will leave an indelible impression on their minds. On the other hand, subjects taught by a teacher who does not show true concern for his or her students' overall well-being will be regarded as temporary and not retained for long.

Similarly, if one is sick and being treated in hospital by a doctor who evinces a warm human feeling, one feels at ease and the doctor's desire to give the best possible care is itself curative, irrespective of the degree of his or her technical skill. On the other hand, if one's doctor lacks human feeling and displays an unfriendly expression, impatience or casual disregard, one will feel anxious, even if he or she is the most highly qualified doctor and the disease has been correctly diagnosed and the right medication prescribed. Inevitably, patients' feelings make a difference to the quality and completeness of their recovery.

Even when we engage in ordinary conversation in everyday life, if someone speaks with human feeling we enjoy listening, and respond accordingly; the whole conversation becomes interesting, however unimportant the topic may be. On the other hand, if a person speaks coldly or harshly, we feel uneasy and wish for a quick end to the interaction. From the least to the most important event, the affection and respect of others are vital for our happiness.

Recently I met a group of scientists in America who said that the rate of mental illness in their country was quite high — around twelve percent of the population. It became clear during our discussion that the main cause of depression was not a lack of material necessities but a deprivation of the affection of others.

So, as you can see from everything I have written so far, one thing seems clear to me: whether or not we are consciously aware of it, from the day we are born, the need for human affection is in our very blood. Even if the affection comes from an animal or someone we would normally consider an enemy, both children and adults will naturally gravitate towards it.

I believe that no one is born free from the need for love. And this demonstrates that, although some modern schools of thought seek to do so, human beings cannot be defined as solely physical. No material object, however beautiful or valuable, can make us feel loved, because our deeper identity and true character lie in the subjective nature of the mind.

Developing compassion

Some of my friends have told me that, while love and compassion are marvelous and good, they are not really very relevant. Our world, they say, is not a place where such beliefs have much influence or power. They claim that anger and hatred are so much a part of human nature that humanity will always be dominated by them. I do not agree.

We humans have existed in our present form for about a hundred thousand years. I believe that if during this time the human mind had been primarily controlled by anger and hatred, our overall population would have decreased. But today, despite all our wars, we find that the human population is greater than ever. This clearly indicates to me that love and compassion predominate in the world. And this is why unpleasant events are "news"; compassionate activities are so much a part of daily life that they are taken for granted and, therefore, largely ignored.

So far I have been discussing mainly the mental benefits of compassion, but it contributes to good physical health as well. According to my personal experience, mental stability and physical well-being are directly related. Without question, anger and agitation make us more susceptible to illness. On the other hand, if the mind is tranquil and occupied with positive thoughts, the body will not easily fall prey to disease.

But of course it is also true that we all have an innate self-centeredness that inhibits our love for others. So, since we desire the true happiness that is brought about by only a calm mind, and since such peace of mind is brought about by only a compassionate attitude, how can we develop this? Obviously, it is not enough for us simply to think about how nice compassion is! We need to make a concerted effort to develop it; we must use all the events of our daily life to transform our thoughts and behavior.

First of all, we must be clear about what we mean by compassion. Many forms of compassionate feeling are mixed with desire and attachment. For instance, the love parents feel for their child is often strongly associated with their own emotional needs, so it is not fully compassionate. Again, in marriage, the love between husband and wife — particularly at the beginning, when each partner still may not know the other's deeper character very well — depends more on attachment than genuine love. Our desire can be so strong that the person to whom we are attached appears to be good, when in fact he or she is very negative. In addition, we have a tendency to exaggerate small positive qualities. Thus when one partner's attitude changes, the other partner is often disappointed and his or her attitude changes too. This is an indication that love has been motivated more by personal need than by genuine care for the other individual.

True compassion is not just an emotional response but a firm commitment founded on reason. Therefore, a truly compassionate attitude towards others does not change even if they behave negatively.

Of course, developing this kind of compassion is not at all easy! As a start, let us consider the following facts:

Whether people are beautiful and friendly or unattractive and disruptive, ultimately they are human beings, just like oneself. Like oneself, they want happiness and do not want suffering. Furthermore, their right to overcome suffering and be happy is equal to one's own. Now, when you recognize that all beings are equal in both their desire for happiness and their right to obtain it, you automatically feel empathy and closeness for them. Through accustoming your mind to this sense of universal altruism, you develop a feeling of responsibility for others: the wish to help them actively overcome their problems. Nor is this wish selective; it applies equally to all. As long as they are human beings experiencing pleasure and pain just as you do, there is no logical basis to discriminate between them or to alter your concern for them if they behave negatively.

Let me emphasize that it is within our power, given patience and time, to develop this kind of compassion. Of course, our self-centeredness, our distinctive attachment to the feeling of an independent, self-existent "I", works fundamentally to inhibit our compassion. Indeed, true compassion can be experienced only when this type of self-grasping is eliminated. But this does not mean that we cannot start and make progress now.

How we can start

We should begin by removing the greatest hindrances to compassion: anger and hatred. As we all know, these are extremely powerful emotions and they can overwhelm our entire mind. Nevertheless, they can be controlled. If, however, they are not, these negative emotions will plague us — with no extra effort on their part! — and impede our quest for the happiness of a loving mind.

So as a start, it is useful to investigate whether or not anger is of value. Sometimes, when we are discouraged by a difficult situation, anger does seem helpful, appearing to bring with it more energy, confidence and determination.

Here, though, we must examine our mental state carefully. While it is true that anger brings extra energy, if we explore the nature of this energy, we discover that it is blind: we cannot be sure whether its result will be positive or negative. This is because anger eclipses the best part of our brain: its rationality. So the energy of anger is almost always unreliable. It can cause an immense amount of destructive, unfortunate behavior. Moreover, if anger increases to the extreme, one becomes like a mad person, acting in ways that are as damaging to oneself as they are to others.

It is possible, however, to develop an equally forceful but far more controlled energy with which to handle difficult situations.

This controlled energy comes not only from a compassionate attitude, but also from reason and patience. These are the most powerful antidotes to anger. Unfortunately, many people misjudge these qualities as signs of weakness. I believe the opposite to be true: that they are the true signs of inner strength. Compassion is by nature gentle, peaceful and soft, but it is also very powerful. It is those who easily lose their patience who are insecure and unstable. Thus, to me, the arousal of anger is a direct sign of weakness.

So, when a problem first arises, try to remain humble and maintain a sincere attitude and be concerned that the outcome is fair. Of course, others may try to take advantage of you, and if your remaining detached only encourages unjust aggression, adopt a strong stand. This, however, should be done with compassion, and if it is necessary to express your views and take strong countermeasures, do so without anger or ill-intent.

You should realize that even though your opponents appear to be harming you, in the end, their destructive activity will damage only themselves. In order to check your own selfish impulse to retaliate, you should recall your desire to practice compassion and assume responsibility for helping prevent the other person from suffering the consequences of his or her acts.

Thus, because the measures you employ have been calmly chosen, they will be more effective, more accurate and more forceful. Retaliation based on the blind energy of anger seldom hits the target.

Friends and enemies

I must emphasize again that merely thinking that compassion and reason and patience are good will not be enough to develop them.

We must wait for difficulties to arise and then attempt to practice them.

And who creates such opportunities? Not our friends, of course, but our *enemies*. They are the ones who give us the most trouble. So if we truly wish to learn, we should consider enemies to be our best teacher!

For a person who cherishes compassion and love, the practice of tolerance is essential, and for that, an enemy is indispensable. So we should feel grateful to our enemies, for it is they who can best help us develop a tranquil mind! Also, it is often the case in both personal and public life, that with a change in circumstances, enemies become friends.

So anger and hatred are *always* harmful, and unless we train our minds and work to reduce their negative force, they will continue to disturb us and disrupt our attempts to develop a calm mind. Anger and hatred are our real enemies. These are the forces we most need to confront and defeat, not the temporary "enemies" who appear intermittently throughout life.

Of course, it is natural and right that we all want friends. I often joke that if you really want to be selfish, you should be very altruistic! You should take good care of others, be concerned for their welfare, help them, serve them, make more friends, make more smiles. The result? When you yourself need help, you find plenty of helpers! If, on the other hand, you neglect the happiness of others, in the long term you will be the loser. And is friendship produced through quarrels and anger, jealousy and intense competitiveness? I do not think so. Only affection brings us genuine close friends.

In today's materialistic society, if you have money and power, you seem to have many friends. But they are not friends of yours; they are the friends of your money and power. When you lose your wealth and influence, you will find it very difficult to track these people down.

The trouble is that when things in the world go well for us, we become confident that we can manage by ourselves and feel we do not need friends, but as our status and health decline, we quickly realize how wrong we were. That is the moment when we learn who is really helpful and who is completely useless. So to prepare for that moment, to make genuine friends who will help us when the need arises, we ourselves must cultivate altruism!

Though sometimes people laugh when I say it, I myself always want more friends. I love smiles. Because of this I have the problem of knowing how to make more friends and how to get more smiles, in particular, genuine smiles. For there are many kinds of smile, such as sarcastic, artificial or diplomatic smiles. Many smiles produce no feeling of satisfaction, and sometimes they can even create suspicion or fear, can't they? But a genuine smile really gives us a feeling of freshness and is, I believe, unique to human beings. If these are the smiles we want, then we ourselves must create the reasons for them to appear.

Compassion and the world

In conclusion, I would like briefly to expand my thoughts beyond the topic of this short piece and make a wider point: individual happiness can contribute in a profound and effective way to the overall improvement of our entire human community.

Because we all share an identical need for love, it is possible to feel that anybody we meet, in whatever circumstances, is a brother or sister. No matter how new the face or how different the dress and behavior, there is no significant division between us and other people. It is foolish to dwell on external differences, because our basic natures are the same.

Ultimately, humanity is one and this small planet is our only home. If we are to protect this home of ours, each of us needs to experience a vivid sense of universal altruism. It is only this feeling that can remove the self-centered motives that cause people to deceive and misuse one another. If you have a sincere and open heart, you naturally feel self-worth and confidence, and there is no need to be fearful of others.

I believe that at every level of society — familial, tribal, national and international — the key to a happier and more successful world is the growth of compassion. We do not need to become religious, nor do we need to believe in an ideology. All that is necessary is for each of us to develop our good human qualities.

I try to treat whoever I meet as an old friend. This gives me a genuine feeling of happiness. It is the practice of compassion.

NEW FROM WISDOM

The definitive book on Tibetan Buddhism by the world's ultimate authority—His Holiness the Dalai Lama of Tibet!

THE WORLD OF TIBETAN BUDDHISM
by Tenzin Gyatso, the Fourteenth Dalai Lama
Translated, edited, and annotated by Geshe Thupten Jinpa
with a foreword by Richard Gere

With characteristic humility, His Holiness the Dalai Lama begins this landmark survey of the entire Buddhist path, saying, "I think an overview of Tibetan Buddhism for the purpose of providing a comprehensive framework of the Buddhist path may prove helpful in deepening your understanding and practice."

"His Holiness offers a clear and penetrating overview of Tibetan Buddhist practice from the Four Noble Truths to Highest Yoga Tantra with, as always, special emphasis on the practice of love, kindness, and universal responsibility."
—*Richard Gere, from the foreword*
240 pp., $14.00   ISBN 0-86171-097-5

Also from Wisdom by the Dalai Lama

THE MEANING OF LIFE FROM A BUDDHIST PERSPECTIVE
Translated and edited by Jeffrey Hopkins
120 pp., illustrations, $12.50   ISBN 0-86171-096-7

MINDSCIENCE: AN EAST-WEST DIALOGUE
with Herbert Benson, Robert A. F. Thurman, Howard E. Gardner, Daniel Goleman, et al.
140 pp., illustrations, $12.50   ISBN 0-86171-066-5

OPENING THE EYE OF NEW AWARENESS
Translated by Donald S Lopez, Jr., with Jeffrey Hopkins
144 pp., $12.95   ISBN 0-86171-036-3

THE KALACHAKRA TANTRA: RITE OF INITIATION
Translated, edited, and introduced by Jeffrey Hopkins
510 pp., color illustrations, cloth $29.95   ISBN 0-86171-093-2

Wisdom can also supply all other books by and about His Holiness the Dalai Lama and a wide range of other books on Buddhism and Tibet.

To order or for more information, contact:
Wisdom Publications, 361 Newbury St, Boston, MA 02115, USA. Toll-free order line (USA only): 1-800-272-4050.
In Australia: **Mandala Books**, 620 Camberwell Rd, Camberwell, Victoria 3124. Telephone: (03) 889-4100. Fax: (03) 889-1200.

Wisdom Publications

Wisdom Publications is a publisher of books on Buddhism, Tibet, and related East-West themes. Our titles are published in appreciation of Buddhism as a living philosophy and with the special commitment to preserve and transmit important works from all major Buddhist traditions. They cover the areas of philosophy, psychology, health, art, science, language, biography, culture, travel and pilgrimage, engaged Buddhism, politics, children's books, and more. If you would like further information, a copy of our mail order catalogue, or news about forthcoming publications, please write or call us at 361 Newbury Street, Boston, Massachusetts 02115, USA. Telephone: (617) 536-3358. Fax: (617) 536-1897.

The Wisdom Trust

As a non-profit publishing charity, Wisdom is dedicated to the publication of fine Dharma books for the benefit of all sentient beings and dependent upon the kindness and generosity of sponsors in order to do so. We have many excellent manuscripts waiting for a benefactor. One hundred per cent of any donation made to the Wisdom Trust Fund will be used exclusively for the project for which it was intended. If you would like to make a contribution to Wisdom to help us continue our Dharma work or to receive information about opportunities for planned giving, please contact our Boston office. Thank you so much.

Wisdom is a tax-deductible 501(c)(3) non-profit organization and the English language publishing division of the Foundation for the Preservation of the Mahayana Tradition.

The Foundation for the Preservation of the Mahayana Tradition

The Foundation for the Preservation of the Mahayana Tradition (FPMT) is an international network of Buddhist centers and activities dedicated to the transmission of Mahayana Buddhism as a practiced and living tradition. The FPMT was founded in 1975 by Lama Thubten Yeshe and Lama Thubten Zopa Rinpoche, and comprises monasteries, retreat centers, communities, publishing houses, and healing centers, all functioning as a means to benefit others. Teachings such as those presented in this book are given at many of these centers.

To receive a complete listing of FPMT centers as well as news about the activities throughout this global network, please write requesting a complimentary copy of the MANDALA journal to: FPMT Central Office, P.O. Box 1778, Soquel, California 95073. Telephone: (408) 476-8435. Fax: (408) 476-4823.

Publisher's Acknowledgments

The publisher gratefully acknowledges the kind help of the following people in sponsoring the publication of this booklet: Rosa Shen, Jack Sonnabaum, Judith Hunt, The Buddhist Library (Sydney), Terry Fralich, Katherine Donovan and Kama Gyalzin Sherpa, Joanne Huang, Grace Su, Lily Or, Ming Hua Chen, Shio-Ying Tsai, Kee-Cheng and Erica Wei, Maria Chen, Margaret Lu, Su-Fen Shih, Angela Wang, Sophia Tsou, Wenyu Trading, Ean Hong Ching, Yen-Hwa Mar, Len-Yi Leu, Linda Rou, Sue Huang, L S Lien and K C Liu, Su-Ming Chan, and the families of Li Ping Zhao, Kenneth K Wu, Kim Hioe, Dwayne Ladle, Chou-Mou Huang, Zimmer Jan, Mike Chuang, Yu Wen Han, Frank G Lin, Gene Kuo, Mei-Nien Shen, Hsiao-Chang Fang, Philip C Cheng, Eric C Kuo, Wun Sen Lin, Eddie Liu, Chain C Hsu, Tsungnan N Chen, Song Chyr Chen, Henry Chen, Dick Lee, Parkson Wong, Chi-Shin Wang, Nelson Kwan, Sing-Shein Yang, John Tsai, Paul Chu, and Tony S Ma.